About the Author™

Meet
Daniel Pinkwater

Alice B. McGinty

The Rosen Publishing Group's
PowerKids Press™
New York

To Daniel

Published in 2003 by The Rosen Publishing Group, Inc.
29 East 21st Street, New York, NY 10010

First Edition

Editor: Frances E. Ruffin
Book Design: Maria E. Melendez

Photo Credits: Cover, title page, pp. 4, 19, 20 © Kathy McLaughlin; pp. 2, 5, 7, 8, 12, 22 courtesy of Daniel Pinkwater.

Grateful acknowledgment is made for permission to reprint previously published material:
p. 10 (sidebar): From LIZARD MUSIC by D. Manus Pinkwater, copyright © 1976 by Manus Pinkwater. Used by permission of G.P. Putnam's Sons, an imprint of Penguin Putnam Books for Young Readers, a division of Penguin Putnam, Inc. All rights reserved.
pp. 11, 18 (sidebar): Reprinted with the permission of Simon & Schuster Books for Young Readers, an imprint of Simon & Schuster Children's Publishing Division from THE HOBOKEN CHICKEN EMERGENCY By D. Manus Pinkwater. Copyright © 1977 D. Manus Pinkwater.
pp. 16, 17 (sidebar): Reprinted with the permission of Atheneum Books for Young Readers, an imprint of Simon & Schuster Children's Publishing Division from RAINY MORNING By Daniel Pinkwater, illustrated by Jill Pinkwater. Text copyright © 1999 Daniel Pinkwater. Illustrations copyright © 1999 Jill Pinkwater.

McGinty, Alice B.
    Meet Daniel Pinkwater / Alice B. McGinty.— 1st ed.
        p. cm. — (About the author)
    Summary: A short biography of the author of more than seventy books for children, Daniel Pinkwater.
    Includes bibliographical references and index.
    ISBN 0-8239-6406-X
    1. Pinkwater, Daniel Manus, 1941– —Juvenile literature. 2. Authors, American—20th century—Biography—Juvenile literature. 3. Young adult fiction—Authorship—Juvenile literature. [1. Pinkwater, Daniel Manus, 1941– 2. Authors, American.] I. Title. II. Series.
    PS3566.I526 Z77 2003
        813'.54—dc21

                                2002000136

            Manufactured in the United States of America

Contents

daniel pinkwater

... Manus Pinkwater was born on November 15, 19.. in Memphis, Ten...

... father who was from Poland, supported the family ...

daniel pinkwater

daniel water

daniel pinkwater

... sed funny notes at school so that his friends would ...

... in trouble. However, Daniel did not want to be a writer. He was ...

The Fantastic Mr. Pinkwater

What do crazy **characters** such as fat men from outer space, music-making lizards, and a 200-pound (91-kg) chicken have in common? They were all made up by the same man, an author named Daniel Manus Pinkwater. Maybe it is because he writes such fantastic stories that some people call him the Fantastic Mr. Pinkwater.

Daniel Pinkwater says that when he writes a story, he thinks about himself as a child. He remembers the tastes, sounds, and feelings that he experienced when he was a boy. Then he writes a book that he would like to have read.

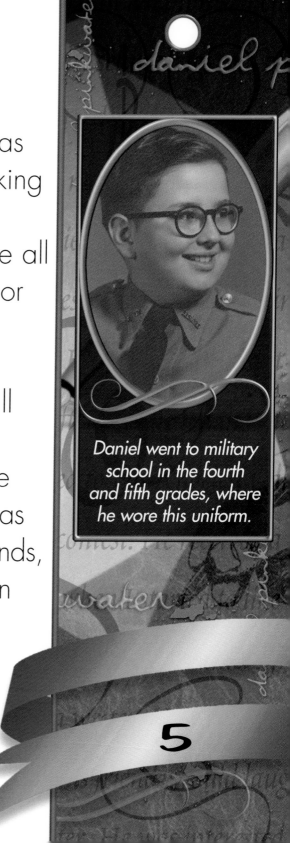

Daniel went to military school in the fourth and fifth grades, where he wore this uniform.

Daniel Pinkwater's first books were written under the name Manus Pinkwater. He later ◀ *wrote books as D. Manus Pinkwater, then Daniel M. Pinkwater. Most of his readers know him as Daniel Pinkwater.*

Beginnings

Daniel Manus Pinkwater was born on November 15, 1941, in Memphis, Tennessee. His father, who was from Poland, supported the family by selling rags and old army boots. Daniel's mother, the daughter of a **rabbi**, had been a dancer. Daniel had two half sisters and two half brothers. His family moved many times. When Daniel was two years old, they moved to Chicago, Illinois. He loved their big apartment in the city and later used the **setting** in many of his stories. Daniel learned to read in the first grade. He bought a *Batman* comic book. He worked hard every day until he could read it all by himself. After that he felt that he could read anything.

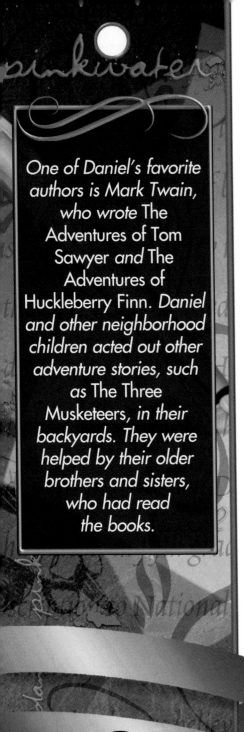

One of Daniel's favorite authors is Mark Twain, who wrote The Adventures of Tom Sawyer and The Adventures of Huckleberry Finn. *Daniel and other neighborhood children acted out other adventure stories, such as* The Three Musketeers, *in their backyards. They were helped by their older brothers and sisters, who had read the books.*

Daniel's father, Felix (left), came to America from Poland. Daniel's grandfather (right) was named ▶ *Manus, which is Daniel's middle name.*

daniel pinkwater

1948

Top: *Eight-year-old Daniel posed for the camera.*
Bottom: *Daniel (bottom row, third from the left) sat with his classmates at Chicago's Nettlehorst School.*

NETTELHORST SCHOOL
OCT 27 1949
ROOM 318

daniel pinkwater

A Budding Writer?

When Daniel was eight, his family moved to Los Angeles, California. While there, in fifth grade, Daniel won a story-writing contest. He received a free **subscription** to *National Geographic* magazine. "That's when I started to like writing," Daniel says. "I found out you can get things. People **respect** you."

Daniel's friends and family always believed that he would grow up to be a writer. He made up funny stories and jokes. However, Daniel did not want to be a writer. He was interested in art. He bought a drawing kit and practiced drawing. He even printed his own photographs.

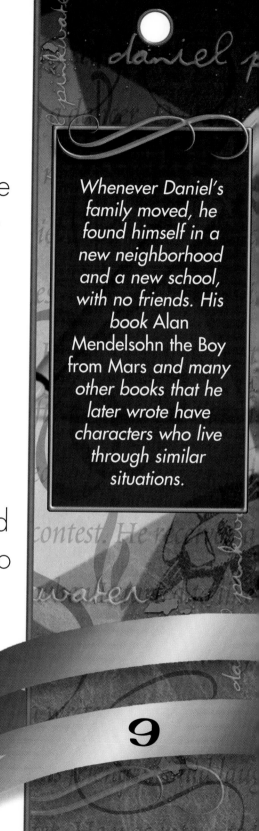

Whenever Daniel's family moved, he found himself in a new neighborhood and a new school, with no friends. His book *Alan Mendelsohn the Boy from Mars* and many other books that he later wrote have characters who live through similar situations.

The Chicken Man

When Daniel was 14, his family moved back to Chicago. Daniel loved Chicago. As a teenager, Daniel began a **pastime** that he still enjoys today. He explores cities. Daniel rode the Chicago buses on their entire routes. He walked miles (km) through the city. He found unusual cafés, movie theaters, comic book stores, and parks in out-of-the-way places. Daniel also saw people who were very unusual. One such person was the Chicken Man. This was a man who dressed in a raincoat and carried a real live chicken under his hat. When the man took off his hat, the chicken danced on the Chicken Man's shoulder and clucked into a toy telephone.

Daniel's wife, Jill, created this art for the cover of Daniel's book The Hoboken ▶ Chicken Emergency.

"I was glad that Leslie wasn't around, what with the lizard and Chicken Man mystery going on. She would probably have gotten hysterical. She doesn't like lizards and snakes and things like that. Probably, she would have started screaming for her mommy, and calling the police, and generally making it impossible to get to the bottom of things. I had an investigation on my hands, and I certainly didn't need my crazy sister to make it harder."
—from p. 50–51, Lizard Music (1976)

THE HOBOKEN CHICKEN EMERGENCY

by Daniel Pinkwater

Illustrated by Jill Pinkwater

A Tall Chicken Tale by
the host of Public Radio's
Chinwag Theater

ALADDIN HUMOR

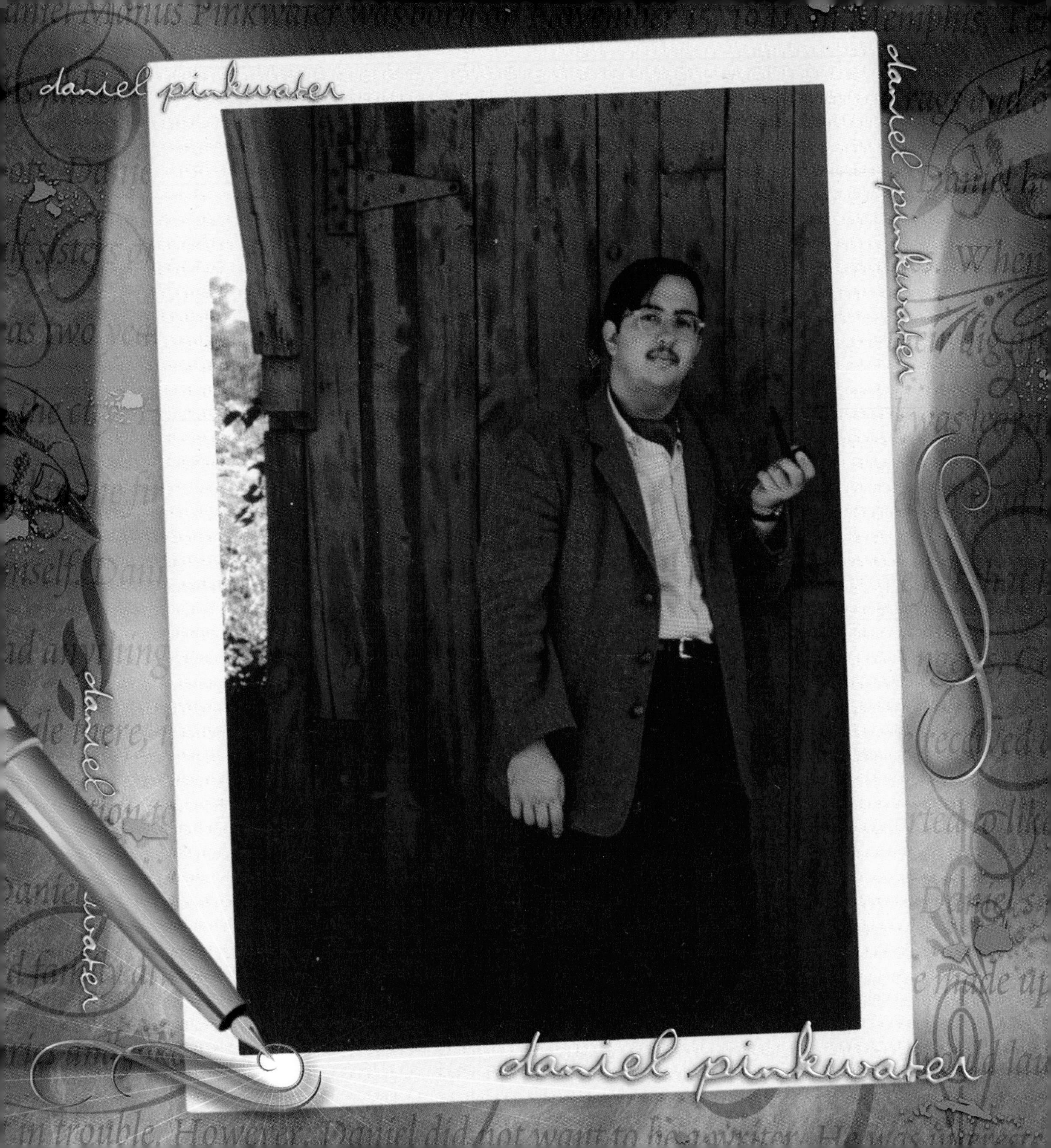

Life as a Sculptor

Daniel attended Bard College in New York State, where he studied many subjects. When his father told him to focus on one subject, Daniel chose art. He wanted to become a **sculptor**. Daniel graduated from Bard in 1964. While in college, he began a three-year **apprenticeship** with a sculptor. When Daniel completed his studies, the sculptor said, "I never thought you'd be a sculptor. I've always thought you'd be a writer." Daniel was surprised and upset by these comments. He was determined to become a sculptor. While he created his art, he earned money by teaching children's art classes.

After college, Daniel moved to Hoboken, New Jersey, just a ferryboat ride across the Hudson River from New York City.

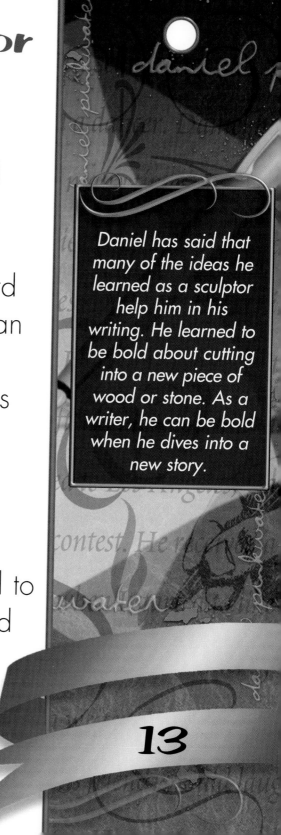

Daniel has said that many of the ideas he learned as a sculptor help him in his writing. He learned to be bold about cutting into a new piece of wood or stone. As a writer, he can be bold when he dives into a new story.

The Terrible Roar

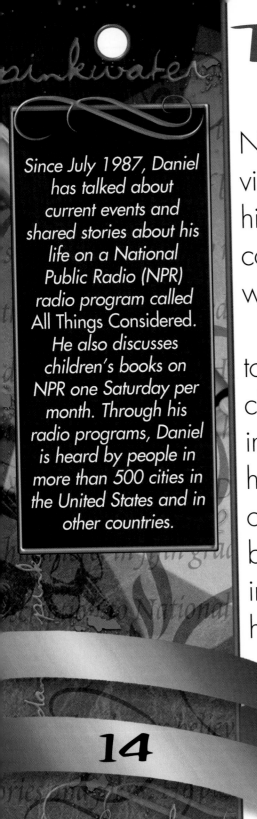

Daniel lived and worked in Hoboken, New Jersey, but he loved to travel. He visited countries around the world. One of his favorite places was **Tanzania**, a country in Africa. During his visit there, he worked and studied with African artists.

After returning from Africa, Daniel went to a party one evening. He met a children's book **editor** there. She was interested in African art. Daniel showed her his African artwork, and she liked it. She offered him a job **illustrating** a children's book. Daniel decided to try it. However, instead of illustrating someone else's story, he wrote his own story to go with the drawings. *The Terrible Roar*, Daniel's first book, was published in 1970.

Many art magazines praised Daniel's illustrations in The Terrible Roar. *A magazine for artists selected* The Terrible Roar *as one of the 100 best children's books.*

As a young man Daniel was serious about his work, but he also enjoyed having fun, as this photo shows.

daniel pinkwater

Changes

Daniel enjoyed writing and illustrating *The Terrible Roar*, but he still wanted to be a sculptor. He was excited when a **woodcut print** that he had created was chosen for an **exhibit** at the Brooklyn Museum. While his print was on exhibit, Daniel noticed that many adults walked past it. The children he taught in his art classes paid much better attention to art. Daniel liked the way children looked at objects, artwork, and the world around them. It was then that Daniel realized he wanted to write and illustrate books for children. Daniel had also gone through another change in his life when he met Jill Miriam Schutz, a teacher. In 1969, Daniel and Jill were married.

In the 1970s, Daniel began to write and illustrate many more books for children. He wrote the book Rainy Morning. *The picture on the opposite page is his wife Jill's illustration from the book.*

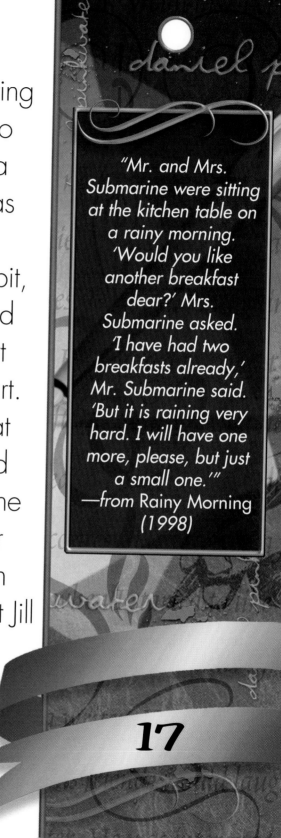

"Mr. and Mrs. Submarine were sitting at the kitchen table on a rainy morning. 'Would you like another breakfast dear?' Mrs. Submarine asked. 'I have had two breakfasts already,' Mr. Submarine said. 'But it is raining very hard. I will have one more, please, but just a small one.'"
—from Rainy Morning (1998)

Daniel and Jill

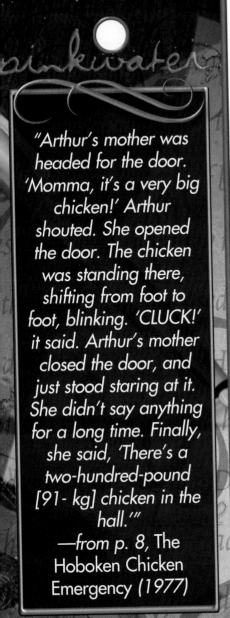

Daniel and Jill have not had children, but they both love animals. Over the years, they have added cats, dogs, and horses to their family. They opened a dog-training school and wrote a dog-training book called *Superpuppy*. Daniel and Jill also work together in another way. One day, Jill read a story of Daniel's that he had not yet illustrated. Jill, who had always liked art, asked if she could try drawing some pictures for the new book. "Sure," Daniel said. When Jill showed him her drawings, Daniel was amazed. He called his **publisher**. "You won't believe this," he said, "but I want my wife to illustrate my picture book." Jill has been illustrating Daniel's books ever since.

Before illustrating Daniel's books, Jill Pinkwater (left) wrote books of her own, including Mr. Fred, ▶ Buffalo Brenda, *and* Cloud Horse.

daniel pinkwater
daniel pinkwater
daniel pinkwater
daniel pinkwater

The Best Is Yet to Come

Daniel Pinkwater has published more than 70 books for children. He is known and loved for his funny, imaginative, truthful way of looking at the world.

Daniel, Jill, and their animals live on an old farm in New York State. When Daniel is not writing, he is walking his dogs, hiking, eating Chinese food, or maybe enjoying a codfish ice-cream cone. Daniel also enjoys answering letters from children who have read his books. When he is asked which is the best book he's ever written, Daniel replies that he hasn't written it yet. That gives his readers a lot to look forward to!

◀ *Daniel may have taken a bit of time off from writing his next book to pose with his friend Jacques.*

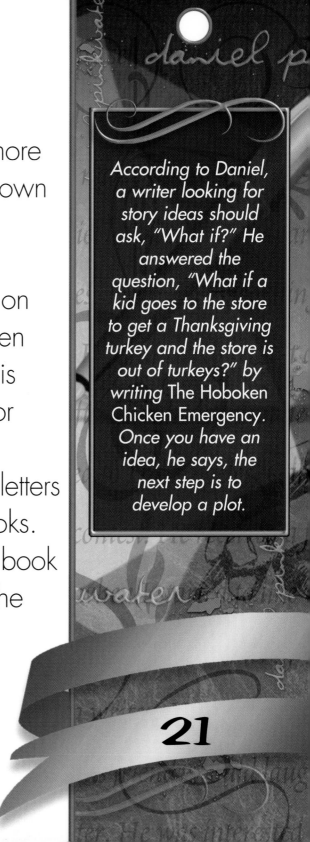

According to Daniel, a writer looking for story ideas should ask, "What if?" He answered the question, "What if a kid goes to the store to get a Thanksgiving turkey and the store is out of turkeys?" by writing The Hoboken Chicken Emergency. *Once you have an idea, he says, the next step is to develop a plot.*

In His Own Words

Daniel Pinkwater, dressed for a cold winter's day.

Why do you like to write for children?
Adults are not as good readers as kids. Kids are great readers.

Why do you like writing?
I can get better and better and better and better at it. I never reach a point where I've gone as far as I can go as a writer.

Do you have a favorite place to write?
I work at a gray metal desk that used to belong to IBM. Before that I had a pink Formica [plastic-topped] table that I got from a Chinese restaurant.

Do you always illustrate your books?
I no longer illustrate my books. My wife, Jill, does it now. She is much better at it than I am.

Did you want to be a writer when you were young?
I never wanted to be a writer. Everyone else wanted me to be a writer. Being a writer didn't seem as exciting as being a cowboy, a movie star, or a yachtsman [with a big boat].

Why do you feel that you have been successful as a writer/illustrator?
I don't feel that I've reached success yet.

Glossary

apprenticeship (uh-PREN-tis-ship) When a young person works with an experienced person to learn a skill or trade.

characters (KAR-ik-turz) The people or animals that appear in a story.

darkroom (DARK-room) A special room for developing photographs.

editor (EH-dih-ter) A person in charge of correcting errors, checking facts, and deciding what will be printed in a newspaper, magazine, or book.

exhibit (ig-ZIH-bit) Objects or pictures set out for people to see.

illustrating (IH-luhs-trayt-ing) Creating pictures that help to explain a story, poem, or book.

pastime (PAS-tym) A hobby or an activity that makes time pass in an enjoyable way.

publisher (PUH-blih-shur) A person or company whose business is printing and selling books, newspapers, or magazines.

rabbi (RA-by) The spiritual leader of a Jewish community.

respect (rih-SPEKT) To think highly of someone or something.

sculptor (SKULP-tur) A person who makes works of art in clay, metal, stone, or wood.

setting (SEH-ting) The time and place in which a story takes place.

subscription (sub-SKRIP-shun) An agreement to pay for and to receive a number of issues of a magazine.

Tanzania (tan-zuh-NEE-uh) A country in eastern Africa.

woodcut print (WUD-kuht PRIHNT) A picture made from rubbing charcoal or other art materials against a wood carving.

Index

Web Sites

Due to the changing nature of Internet links, PowerKids Press has developed
an online list of Web sites related to the subject of this book. This site is
updated regularly. Please use this link to access the list:
www.powerkidslinks.com/aa/danpinkw/